Divine Guidance

The Answers You Need to
Make Miracles ...

Divine Guidance

The Answers You Need to Make Miracles ...

Stephanie J. King

BOOKS

Winchester, UK
Washington, USA

First published by Sixth Books, 2013
Sixth Books is an imprint of John Hunt Publishing Ltd., Laurel House, Station Approach,
Alresford, Hants, SO24 9JH, UK
office1@jhpbooks.net
www.johnhuntpublishing.com
www.6th-books.com

For distributor details and how to order please visit the 'Ordering' section on our website.

A CIP catalogue record for this book is available from the British Library.

Design: Stuart Davies

Printed and bound by CPI Group (UK) Ltd, Croydon, CR0 4YY

We operate a distinctive and ethical publishing philosophy in all
areas of our business, from our global network of authors to
production and worldwide distribution.

For all...
To birth Heaven realistically upon Earth
that miracles can indeed be physically present
in a divine conscious and connected way...

(I am I) In the beginning man was able to speak easily. Then the connection was halted through misunderstanding and fear. Mankind wrongly believed himself to be abandoned and alone on a planet of birth and decay, regardless of efforts to be otherwise. I have always been aware of this, for the link that we share exists for life. Each soul is on a progressive journey of growth, exploration and contribution. Each is individual yet linked eternally with me, through the process of living and life itself. (I am I)

Foreword

How can I explain the work of Stephanie J. King – except brilliant? Everything she does, she does with Spirit. Every word she speaks is channelled too. For many years she has dedicated her life to unlocking the potential of others, young and old, rich or poor. She works for the highest realms to empower and spur people on - to work on their own soul agenda, to access talents, gifts and strengths they possess, to stir latent potential for the good of their own life and purpose and for the greater good of the greater whole - the realms of Earth and Heaven as they combine.

Every soul alive has karma to work through. Stephanie will not only help you recognise and work through it, but she'll elevate your state of consciousness for the remainder of the time that you are here. Her latest book works the same - only now ask a question - any question - and the answer will immediately be presented, like with a direct line - a telephone link - to what you need to know or work through now - this very moment. Nothing is beyond your ability to achieve. Stephanie J. King will unlock your potential and zest for living - whatever your soul purpose and presenting path...

Jacky Newcomb multi-award winning and Sunday Times bestselling author of 'An Angel By My Side'.

Introduction

(I am I) What is truth, until it is recognised and fully lived? What is the point of life without the knowledge and understanding through experience that goes with it? (I am I)

For millennia we have believed ourselves separate, self-contained, operating independently from one another and from every other species and life form. But now we are discovering and even proving that this is not completely the whole true picture. We do indeed operate as separate, free-thinking individuals, but we also continue to invent and interlink with the planet's own intelligence, with the real-time creative life force that's working with and through us on many levels. Whether we want it to, whether we realise it or not, nothing slips past this invincible power unnoticed.

Life operates on many different levels simultaneously, and so do people. What we see occurring on the surface is often just a fragment of a whole unfolding saga playing out. We are driven by emotions, perception, intention, needs and wants. Things we think and feel can chop and change within an instant, depending on desire and perspective. If we had the gift of hindsight before events occurred, we would be more equipped to know exactly what was called for through our input; we'd pay life forward. What we really seek is wisdom, better insight and higher knowledge that can aid us in our tasks at the very moment in actual time that things present.

Miracles are an everyday occurrence from the most ordinary to quite profound, but they slip easily past unnoticed and therefore ungratified. *Divine Guidance* brings them back into conscious alignment and reality, in a way that helps Earth's own thriving intelligent creative life force work with you.

You form part of life, which works through you. All you say, think and do crops up somewhere. All things interlink through Earth's own active web of conscious energy; a vital, thriving, intelligent force that envelopes and permeates the planet. What we each experience is but a segment of what's occurring collectively. What we sense is often a fraction of what's actually going on, for every situation that presents has at least two sides. *Divine Guidance* highlights what we don't always see clearly or easily ourselves, like a personal truth mirror or a two way conversation would reveal. Remember that we are linking back to Source here and working with Creation, to help every highest possible outcome come to pass.

Everyone knows the thoughts they think, the life they've lived and what they see, feel, want and need, but few have blazing talents to know their 'soul agenda', to see karma working out, to read the underlying factors that drive life and other people here and now. Few interpret what they see the way it is. If we could be a little more open with intentions, thoughts and feelings, others would read us better and life would flourish. But often we are guarded, our mind is busy somewhere else. We project our inner world through expectation and presumption onto things that are unfolding around us. We colour and misinterpret much of what we witness (hear, think, feel or see). We misread simple signs and signals and often alter, change and colour those we send.

If people everywhere are doing the same thing life is easily muddled, deeds and words get misconstrued, and we misinterpret unseen factors playing out. Presumption, expectation, needs, wants, emotions, feelings, hormones and swinging moods shape some of the many driving factors of how we think and then respond. What we 'think' we see and know can sometimes lead us into trouble because we act on just half the version of perceived events. Yet life is multi-faceted with windows, levels, requirements and purpose, sometimes way beyond what we would ordinarily consider or encounter. At times there may even be 'soul' tasks playing out.

All planetary life forms link and interact together to weave a web of continuous conscious energy and life. Nothing is secluded;

all work and blend as one, simultaneously sparking and igniting with and against each other, producing pockets of activity on creative levels, often invisibly.

(I am I) I second this. Even though seemingly independent, no one and nothing operates alone. All conscious working minds link telepathically and energetically to each other. Every atom of life on earth links back to me. (I am I)

•

Divine Guidance is designed to work with you in the unfolding drama of your life story. It links to higher conscious mind through your own intelligence, through your energetic life force and higher self, linking with and through your Guardian straight to Source/God/Earth/the Universal Source of Life that links to all. This book will take you by the hand to steer you through what is occurring to lead you forward, supporting, advising, to help you achieve the highest outcome available at any moment.

This life is not by accident but personal choice. It is the road map of the live journey your soul is travelling. You can chop and change direction, rethink, re-choose, delay and alter all you wish, for you have the leading character role in your own life story. Nothing sits beyond your capability to achieve. You have the power and vital life force of this planet running through you, helping you to succeed and spurring you on, for its own sake too. Nothing is set in stone until you personally make it so; the future is as pliable as plastic. It can shape shift, flex and change. It actually alters all the time, for every moment contains possibilities yet untapped. You are the activator of what is now and what will be, so it naturally falls to you to do this well.

From your first breath to your last you provide life with live signals, you programme, repel, attract, project what will then be put in motion, though you may not always consciously realise it at the time. You have free choice, deduction and free will. You work with what you know and what you think, believe and want, but so

4

do other people. Every soul alive has a life agenda to accomplish; all have needs to meet and routes to travel.

For life to work with you to its greatest capability, all aspects and all levels must work in sync. What you believe must be the truth and what is desired must synchronise with live events, i.e. raw creative energy, the corresponding truth of others involved, your own attachment to the moment, the physicality of your attention, intent, desire, thought, action, drive and timing must all correctly blend together to align the moment being lived.

This synchronisation of live events is necessary to create the fertile setting for any miracle to occur. Like a well-rehearsed plan or play, all participating pieces join together in the moment 'now' to complete the movement and finished product in fractal time.

Yet given the complexity of this occurrence it is surprisingly simple when conditions are correctly set in place for this to happen. Each moment we experience is often just one long integrated segment of a whole unfolding picture playing out, incorporating other people, situations, circumstance, agendas, aspirations, goals, soul overview, higher purpose etc.

While still in the realms of spirit, before our time of birth, we had a life plan. We saw how life would be on earth today. We knew what we would accomplish, our talents, gifts and strengths, we knew our weaknesses and our downfalls, what we'd contribute, would encounter and could change. We worked out a plan of action of what, how, where, when and why it would apply, we teamed with others who'd birth with us (to form our soul group) along the way. For reasons of their own plan, to work through karma and gain personal growth, to aid the planet and to assist us in contribution and development we'd be a team.

Much we chose ourselves - our location, timing, birth, our parents, siblings, peers, character development and traits, tasks and obstacles to overcome and things that through experience would strengthen, mould, inspire, teach and spur us on. Nothing ever happens of its own accord without a reason. Everything has a purpose and a function. Everything is birthed at some point by someone; every want, desire, and need begins somewhere.

We work and link with life on many intricate levels, but only focus and act upon whatever occurs within the scope of present attention. Yet attention wanders frequently; it dwells on future and past, it's prone to wander when bored or faced with repetition, worry or stress. Very rarely is it functioning and fully present here and now, plus what we take on board can sometimes belong to others with whom we mix.

Understanding the bigger picture always offers an advantage to the situation or live task that's playing. out. Every soul alive has karma to work through. Each is on a personal journey of soul progression and contribution. Each directly channels their own live energy charge or personal life force to the planet. Each must navigate correctly through ongoing effects and cause that correspond directly to actions set in life.

Whenever a soul can distance itself egotistically from daily trials, it will more likely reach triggers and targets for personal accomplishment. Greater happiness, health, contentment, peace, awareness, hope, serenity and a heightened ability to give and receive unconditional love are just a few of the many benefits for it to gain.

You are a working channel for life to flow both to and from. You have your own intelligence, but life does too. In an ideal world all aspects work together in harmony and in sync for you have Life's Source and creativity at your disposal. *Divine Guidance* is designed to help you understand and then command this two-way process, by right of birth.

(I am I) In the beginning it was natural and automatic for humankind to work with me. With tools like these we can rekindle this mutual process. It is now time to realign the way we blend and work together, to help Heaven and Earth combine for mutual benefit. (I am I)

Author's notes

- This work is a three-way link between your self, your guardian and God/Source.
- Any reference to 'man' in this book is the universal word for humanity, for mankind as a whole. It is not intended to place the male gender over or above the female. They are equal.
- All writing by 'I am I' is channelled directly from God; from the Universal Earth/Mind Energy Source. All communicate and connect directly with you, here and now.

For more information, visit www.stephaniejking.com

Preface

We physically live the miracle of life on this living, breathing planet every day. We have free choice and free will. We have the ability to love and grow, to move in any direction and to climb the highest heights that we can dare. Yet how often are we free to feel completely happy?

When we are able to let go of our doubts, something magical begins to happen. Life shifts to another gear. It begins to give us what we thought we could never have. It works with and for us on our behalf. This is only the beginning of the shift that comes to pass; the rest is put in place at the exact time it is needed. All we have to do is to recognise and allow it.

Before our time of birth we were in the realms of spirit, communicating and connecting more with God, with Source and with life. We were more able to trust the process for dualities were not in place; dualities of the ego and the mind. Every soul alive is eternal. During its existence it will experience everything, only then can it really know life's true meaning.

Miracles are not the stuff of myth and legend; they're an everyday occurrence from ordinary to quite profound. They are not things of magic but more life's own helping hand, to put in place what comes to pass for the highest good. They are evidence of the original big bang theory still playing out, the raging battle between positive over negative vibrations, and we ourselves have primary roles in this enfoldment.

Every soul alive is individual yet linked eternally with Source, God, and earth itself. Each is on a journey of discovery and self-improvement. Everyone has karma, tasks to hone or overcome. Each is on the level of attainment earned to date throughout the many different lifetimes of its existence. Each is physical on earth today for its own reason. Throughout this present life time, souls may advance or remain static. Some will reach fulfilment, some will not, depending on its ability to read life, people, situations and circumstance, to connect and interact with the bigger picture that is unfolding through what is put in place by physical action.

(I am I) In the beginning, man and I could converse consciously and directly. Yet this trait was sadly lost throughout the eons of his own evolvement. Through fear, misalignment, misjudgement and wrong thinking, negative belief has incorrectly taught him that he stood alone. (I am I)

We are rediscovering truths today that we thought were lost. Science is even proving that we directly programme life and that life in its turn, through intuition, responds directly back. Animals have never lost this talent; we just wrongly believed we were separate. We thought ourselves sealed units of bone and skin, connecting only through the physical, through deeds, emotions, feelings, actions and spoken words.

We are an intelligent species. We have a wealth of knowledge and information continuously at our disposal that we may not always recognise or access automatically. Every moment in existence is ripe with opportunity to create, connect, contribute, and assist or to make instant change. To offer truths or gain upliftment, to right what's clearly out of sync or visibly wrong, to help life as the greater whole on its movement forward.

It is only in life's physical stage (i.e. physically here and now upon the planet) that change is made solid and permanent. It is only in life's 'now' that the potential and full power of creation is harnessed physically. It is only through the 'now' that creation can continue, for past and future in terms of reality do not exist, but for the eternal, unfurling, unending, continuous moment of *now*.

If we are linked with life and life in its turn links back with us, then it's only natural that both parties can communicate. If we were just purely physical all we must do would fall to us. But we are not; we are beings of intelligent conscious energy that constitute physical matter. We play our part to form the planet that we link with and live upon. When we deliberately interact and link back to the conscious whole we access help. Life itself is easier, lighter and much freer; we are more aware. We connect with higher truths and guidance that reside there for us to be aided by, and to help the conscious shift of humanity evolve forward.

'I am the light' means that the intelligent life force of Source is active within us every moment. Intelligence is energy and energy is light. We each link directly with creation, with the Conscious thinking Mind of Source, God, the planets creative intelligence and life itself. We each carry truth, wisdom and higher knowledge always, at all times, actively within us. We directly access the raw creative intelligence of earth.

'I am the truth' means we have access to the highest truth at every moment. We can know exactly what is needed and what must be put in place as life unfolds. But to gain this information and recognise it fully, consciously, and correctly, we must still clamouring emotions and unnecessary thoughts that chop and change within. We must remain unbiased and completely open to the moment that is presenting and playing out.

'I will lead you through the valley of death' relates to the journey of the soul during physical life and what lies beyond. This does not just mean physical death because death is a natural transition, it is automatic; each soul knows its way home very well for we've made the journey before, we automatically transcend to the place from whence we originally came or to the level that has been earned through this present life time. Being lead through the valley of death also relates to periods of darkness, stress and turmoil, through negative thinking, pain, suffering, loss and misshapen belief while living upon Earth today.

In our darkest, saddest, most fearful hours, as well as in our better ones, we will be taken by the hand and lead forward into peace, balance, understanding, light and love, to feel safe and sound. It means that we can always access what is needed to assist the moment playing out for its highest outcome, no matter what is happening to what or whom, how good or bad.

Each new day we witness is exactly that. It's a blank, clear, open space that we can write upon or programme as we see fit, meaning that we really do hold the key to our entire destiny and life firmly within our own grasp at all times, that we are not always the victims of circumstance that we think.

At every moment two trains of thought, two options are always in existence for us to choose between - positive or negative, light or dark. Light refers to truth, to balance, peace and love, to the bottom line of what's occurring; all other thoughts reflect varying shades of darkness such as jealousy, doubt and fear, stress and thoughts of lack, low confidence and self-esteem and the unending kaleidoscope of negativities that exist. That's all there is.

All we do and all we are fit into one category or the other; if like attracts like then we are either in the positive or the negative at any moment. Every act followed through from this point forward adds live energy to matter and to form. The reality we each experience stems from this. All experiences are created in exactly this same manner, from waves of energy, light and dark that we produce and give life and meaning to, either consciously or not, for the whole of the time span that we exist here.

(I am I) To make life work and to take it forward each person must become more aware of the thoughts and behaviour patterns he naturally generates. Every passing moment he actively attracts and creates his version of the world that he surveys. All he does in his own life he adds to the world as a whole - he adds and computes this to me as his own take on reality and what life means. (I am I)

Each day remains unwritten until you give it meaning, charge and substance. You give reality to what you choose to think about. To be within the love means that you operate from truth and light: By remaining there consistently, consciously, you send balance, peace and healing to troubled areas of the world as they appear.

(I am I) You are helping to disperse the fear and darkness for your own life, for friends and loved ones, for strangers and for me. (I am I)

At least two options, two views, are always available to every question, choice, decision or presenting moment. Divine Guidance will take you by the hand and guide you through them, easily and precisely in a way that resonates with where you are.

How to Use This Book

Divine Guidance is a direct soul-to-soul link to advice for you straight from Source, from your own Guardian/Angel/Guide each time you use it. It will help you work with the 'real-time' language of life's own signs and signals that exist and interlink, often on unseen levels, every day. At random, ask a question and get an answer by opening any page of the book. You will be led straight to information that will prove relevant to you from the very first time that you use it.

Because you know everything about yourself, your thoughts, situations and events, each time you pick it up *Divine Guidance* will connect to your now and be precise in the guidance, words and knowledge being given. It will completely turn around, rebalance and correct many things you both consciously and subconsciously do. This book has the potential to enhance the rest of your life - for the rest of the time frame that you live here - for you'll be working and interacting directly with Source.

Place the book between your palms and let yourself relax. Let your Angel/Guardian/ Guide step forward to communicate; this is a natural process. Keep a question in mind or think about what it is that you need to clarify or know. Take a few long, deep breaths - in through your nose and out through your mouth. Allow your eyes to close as you relax.

(I am I) I will add my energy too. Through this action you will naturally relax further. (I am I)

With your eyes still shut, allow all fears and worries to subside. Shuffle through the pages for as long as you like (if on a Kindle, scroll up and down repeatedly), and at a time you feel inclined, simply stop. With the book still in a closed position, fan through it once again to find the place that you feel drawn. Then read the words that you see written upon the page on which you land.

Life is a challenge for everyone at some time, but the key to its success is our response. If we read the signs correctly we can pass turmoil unscathed, but if we make a wrong decision we add to what is brewing and alter the live dynamics playing out. At times like these we work against the grain. We/life must then work that much harder to set things straight.

Divine Guidance offers what is needed at the specific time that we need help, from teenage onwards. Channelled words and personal insights are spoken straight from Source at a level that links your purpose and your soul with what's at hand. Access higher truths and information: love, work, family, friendships, home. Like an all-seeing oracle, *Divine Guidance* will help you work in tune with life, to help you integrate with creativity and karma playing out. All decisions that you make are always your free choice, but when you know the bigger picture, life is easier.

(I am I) Even though you may not know it, at all times I am with you. But to help you I must speak more easily with you on your level. Miracles are not new; they have always been a part of daily life, not on the scale spoken of in biblical texts, but on a scale that helps effectively with where you are right now. When you let me work with you, we will work as one. Fears will fall away, worst scenarios will too, for they will be a fraction of the size you thought they would be, if indeed they remain at all. You might not always be aware of how powerful you are and that through love, truth,

insight and a humble, open heart you have the healing energy of my Life Force as your aid. You are an intelligent, live extension of me. (I am I)

Be still at this time;
let the answers you seek come to you.
What exists at this moment is different
to what will be in a while.
Sit tight and let things unfold.

*

Life is the pearl in your oyster.
So live it, enjoy it - seize the day!

*

Everything about you is unique,
so make sure you are happy with everything.

*

From this very moment the rest of your life is unfolding.
Pay attention, notice changes, and use them well.

*

Don't let others pull you off track;
they are simply deep in their own 'now' experience.
Remain small and let all storms pass by.

*

Take a long breath and come back
to the peace within your own centre.
When you find it you'll be ready to continue.

*

Life is helping you. Take a moment, trust and go with it.

*

You already know the answer.
Let it unfold; work with it until you reach the next step.

*

Take the path with the best outcome for you, and for life,
based upon where you are at this moment.
You can always re- draw again later.

*

Creativity must flow - so flow with it!

There is no time like the present, so use it to its greatest potential.

*

Good ideas flow towards you for a reason.
Don't let them fade, fester and die without acknowledgement.

*

Forward movement is not possible at this moment,
so stay ready and, for now, bide your time.

*

Money is the currency of this physical world.
Energy is the currency of life: waste neither.

*

Your accomplishments will go with you to the next phase of life,
so be sure you are happy with them all.
If not, then re-draw and re-choose.

*

You are Spirit here and now on an earthly life journey.
You are living a real-time experience.
Enjoy and embrace every second that unfolds,
for when it's over you might wish it were not.

*

Clutter chokes body, space, energy and mind.
Clear away what today's problems are highlighting.
Once you have, you'll be free to move on.

*

Now is prone to time, shift and change.
Move quickly before things move on.

*

Life need not be hard.
Stop, reassess and find a fresh angle to work from.

*

Pay attention to advice.
Know your bottom line and choose for yourself what to apply.

Life is unfolding and evolving through you.
Be sure it's in a way that you'll be proud to own up to -
for nothing is hidden from the soul's point of view.

*

Your dreams, hopes and thoughts are unaccomplished achievements. Don't let them gather dust unfulfilled.

*

Life is short, time is precious.
Make sure you portray how you care. Close your eyes.
Find your central inner space and sit with it for a while.
What you now feel and sense is your personal essence.
It's your personal contribution to the whole.

*

You attract what you give your live energy to,
so be mindful of where your thoughts roam.

*

Keep your eye on the solution and not on the problem.
Allow all efforts to flow in that direction.

*

Happiness is available to all, so let it in.

*

Don't you know that you are perfect as you are?
Be still - and wait.

*

Your life joins with greater life.
Both create and express through all you do. Guide it well.

*

When opportunity knocks, recognise it,
accept it and work with it to see where it leads.
Not everything that glitters is wholesome, good or gold.
Look carefully at what's before you; check again.

*

Miracles do happen.

Think the best, not the worst,
and life will follow.

*

Your mind is a reservoir of knowledge,
so keep it clear.

*

God is on everyone's side.
You just need to listen more carefully.

*

Don't repeat mistakes of the past.
Use today as a point to go forward.

*

Listen carefully;
what you need is about to turn up.

*

Loose ends are an energy drain,
so complete projects and tasks that are waiting.

*

Life's Energies are fertile,
so move forward and stop wasting time.

*

You are a powerful force whether, negative or positive.
Be mindful of which one you choose.

*

Time passes, things change, but fundamentally
all things and all people stay the same.

*

Thoughts are live energy charges.
Be watchful of those you dish out.

*

Expect nothing for only then can you be pleasantly surprised.
If you will work with life then life will work with you.
Joined together you will build and move mountains.

Each person is living their own version of life.
Be selective about what you choose to take on board.

*

No one can live your life for you.
If you're lost, find your way.
If you're down, work out why.
You alone are in charge of this outcome.

*

Miracles occur on many levels,
from the little unexpected ones to the really quite profound.
Be sure you stay aware throughout the day.

*

Become aware of things you do without thinking,
as you may be curbing yourself
from what you most need at this time.

*

Today is a new day with a merit and a tune of its own.
Don't work it all out or stick rigidly to plans,
but instead let new input flow in.

*

What do you need? What are you lacking?
Where are you, or where should you be heading?
Work these things out and direct your answers
in thought-form back to me. (I am I)

*

Time cannot be brought back or repeated again.
It's too valuable to drain away without use.
Remain aware of the many ways that you use it.

*

When you are troubled, I am with you.
When you are sad and lonely, I am there.
Send thoughts such as these directly up to me, so that I
can remove them and give you renewed strength and peace.
Then carry on as usual with your day. (I am I)

Nothing is too hard for you to do.
Remove all negative thoughts and get down to it.

*

Life is not hope-less, but hope-full. Things are not getting worse.
Instead, they are turning around. A pimple must burst
before it can heal and so it's the same with my body;
this living, intelligent planet Earth. (I am I)

*

As a bright, vibrant, sentient being,
don't cloak yourself in darkness, worry, doubt and fear.
Let it go; seize the day, and move on.

*

In the beginning there was nothing but the void.
Now the void is full, it teams with life.
The greatest life of all is this living planet Earth.
You are on it; you form part of it;
you experience it, live it, and breathe it
every waking day of your existence.

*

I love you with all that I am. I trust you with all of my life.
You must learn to love you too - trust in you the way I do.
Now walk forward, straight and tall with this knowledge. (I am I)

*

Mistakes belong in the past, not the present.
Be aware of the choices you make.

*

Each new day that you awake, hand it up to me so that I can guide and
help you gain its merit and greatest outcome possible. (I am I)

*

What you think you can achieve, I will enhance.
What you give your energy to I will match and help you do.
With heart and soul we'll work together to lift mountains. (I am I)

The feelings you have inside at this very moment
are proof that I am with you here and now.
I will find more proof over time to give you,
to show that I am with you, that I am real. (I am I)

*

Life is not a chapter; it's eternal and unending.
Every decade, every century is a passing phase.
Be mindful of the state you'll leave behind you on the planet
for you may come back again to what you weave.

*

Everything you think and do
computes to energy that flows to me.
I in turn transmute it; send it back to then help you.
Such is the flow, the give and take of daily life. (I am I)

*

If someone is angry, send them love and healing thoughts.
Don't take on board as yours what they are feeling.

*

How can you know what this day will bring
when you haven't experienced it yet?
Stop preconditioning. Enjoy it instead.

*

Who will you believe?
Those who have yet to awaken…or me? (I am I)

*

You are more than you understand
or realise at this time.
Life is working with you.
Remain centred in the life force that you own.

*

You have a life agenda, contributions and a destiny to fulfil.
Be the best that you can be and nothing less.

When others let you down, don't cry, moan, stress or fret.
Just reassess the situation and move forward.

*

The life that you now know is only part of a bigger picture;
it contributes and diverges with the rest.
The life role that you possess is important,
so play it well,
for it directs and helps create life's greater whole.

*

Negativity appears when you least expect it,
if not from you then from others in your space.
As soon as you recognise or feel its presence,
send it out in thought form directly back to me
to be recycled, and then move on. (I am I)

*

Your time and deliberate attention, when given freely,
equate to love. Love is the single most precious gift that you
can give. Place it wherever you can for as long as you live.

*

You trust other people far more often than you trust yourself.
You know exactly what you need, and so do I.
Return to your centre point in the heart area of your being.
Let worries dissipate and let life in. (I am I)

*

Retaliation, hate and anger are a futile waste of time,
for they will bounce back even stronger and cling to you.
Cause and effect always ensures that what goes out comes
bouncing back. There is no need for you to add to these things
too.

*

For the next few years we have a unique opportunity to sort out
and clear old rubbish. Take this chance and hasten with it,
before life and opportunity shift again.

The world will not end without man, but without man
who will understand, love, learn, experience and explore.
Earth does need man, but man needs the Earth even more. (I am I)

*

When you don't know what to do,
sit tight and for now do nothing.
Let life unfold a little more.*
Every decision you chose was right at the time that you chose it.
With the aid of hindsight you'll choose again, albeit differently.

*

Not all that you know have you had to live and endure.
Be glad for the knowledge of life and of others around you.

*

Your soul is unique; your journey is too.
Know that you came here for a very good reason.
Find it and live true to your purpose.

*

Ego can be strong, silent, cunning
and appear to fulfil every need.
Don't get caught up in the web
of your own desire or making.

*

In your need to do what's best remain innocent, calm and open.
Return to the bottom line and start again.

*

God is everywhere; in all things and in everyone.
Take all available information into due consideration.
Trust that all you need will come to you.

*

In the beginning I had no one. Now I have man.
For the rest of your life, know you are important to me. (I am I)

To keep hold of all you deem most dear,
be prepared to let it go.
Loosen its grip and connection over you.
Reassess the situation, unbiased and freely.

*

The smallest role played on the stage of real life
might carry the most weight and importance.
Judge no one. Honour all.
Respect every other life as you would respect your own.

*

In the power of now I am with you,
and in this truth lies the full power of life. (I am I)

*

Words perish and fade over time.
You will not. I will not.
I will never leave your calls and needs unanswered. (I am I)

*

Not everything in life can be easy,
but for the enhancement of life
is what everything in life is for.

*

Who are you? What drives the life you're living? God does.
Even though you might lose your way from time to time,
God knows you exactly,
for all that lies behind all of your facets.

*

I think, so therefore I am.
Be positive, aware and focused in your efforts.

*

Empty your head and your thought space.
When the passage is clear more can flow through to assist you.

Life is a paradox; nothing is pre-written.
Yet all is already known and understood.
This life you are living
you created step by step along the way.
Yet you knew where it would lead,
how things would be for yourself and for others,
long before your present birth came to be.

*

Don't look forward or back.
Focus on all present tasks that sit before you, here and now.

*

To pull your life back together, rely on no one but yourself.

*

Keep the solution in focus, not the problem.

*

Assess properly where you are, tie and tidy all loose ends,
then get busy with the real live task of living.

*

Your best is good enough for life and it's good enough for God.
So make sure it really is your best you're giving.

*

Where you are and where you should be
are not too far apart,
but more steps must yet unfold between the two.
Let life and time interplay a little more and
remain safe in the knowledge that you'll get there.

*

To disconnect from earth and life would be impossible.
You chose specifically to be here,
to complete your present life plan and soul agenda.
With strengths and talents that you possess and
the help of a living God,
take up your personal challenge and task of living!

Life can't always provide instant results.
Be patient for things to connect.

*

When you feel happy and whole, life works with you and
flows through you with ease.

*

Be sure everything you give out is for the highest good always,
for natural law insists that what you freely choose to give
always must come back much increased.
You have the power to overwrite your DNA.
Your mindset continuously updates
and re-programmes your body's cells
through information and emotions
you originate, believe and carry.
Be mindful of what you choose to hold on to.

*

Ask and it will be given;
not necessarily in the way you expect,
but in the best way possible at this time.

*

You have the power to make or break this situation.
Let preconditioning and preconceptions fall away.
Remain neutral in your thoughts; add nothing more,
thus allowing God and life to do the rest.

*

To pray is to communicate with me, mind to mind.
Meditation, contemplation, peaceful mind and flowing thought
allow my answers in response to filter through.
So listen, hear, feel, notice, see. (I am I)

*

You are the offering and contribution you give to life!

One day you'll surely know that I am truly with you.
Let today be the day that this begins. (I am I)

*

Life is very simple.
It knows nothing; it is nothing until it is given meaning.
Become aware of the meaning that you give it.

*

On this day, what will you do?
How will it be written to your life's log?

*

Life links us directly; me to you, and you to me. (I am I)

*

Before you were born you existed in Spirit form.
You came to love, express and explore.
But also to help others contribute and make a difference.
From today, use your time and talents to achieve this.

*

You are the eyes and ears of life now.
From your personal vantage point
you will see and know a lot.
Pass as much as you are able
up to Spirit for intervention,
so that more insights, help and guidance
can filter back.

*

Nothing will change until you change it.
With kindness and love begin to set things in motion,
and upon your request I will help you. (I am I)

*

Each child is born innocent, blank, open and new.
Today be again like the child that you once were,
innocent and without preconception.
Let life unfold around you.

You have complete control
of your own life and final outcome.
You are responsible for all
your actions, thoughts and deeds.
From today live according to this knowledge.

*

Truth is constant, enduring, and unchanging.

*

Earth is my body, my physical form. Everything done to it is done to me.
What man does to man, he does to me. (I am I)

*

A mountain has many pathways.
Not all are easy, and some lead nowhere,
but with perseverance it is possible to reach the peak.
Don't stop now, keep going.
With one foot in front of the other,
I'll help you get there myself. (I am I)

*

You have altered and changed a lot throughout your life time.
Don't dither or stagnate, keep on going.*
The smallest step will aid you most at this time. (I am I)

*

Whatever you believe you can be,
when you work with me,
I'll take you higher.
For all that is achieved through me
is much increased. (I am I)

*

Don't walk the same path automatically every day,
whether in thought or in deed.
Take a new one; try a different approach,
allow fresh air and new ideas to filter through.

The world is on the brink of salvation or disaster.
Which one will emerge to win is up to us.
*

When you are presented
with a chance to change or do good
embrace it.
Take the challenge, for if you don't,
can't or won't -
then who will?
*

Life is knocking at your door with good reason.
Assess the opportunity and go with it.*
When you employ every day to its highest capability,
before long you'll look back in pleasure
at what is accomplished.
*

When faced with another's adversity
be still, add nothing.
Allow the moment to take its course,
and silently in your thoughts ask for help.
When again things shift and change
you'll get ample chance to speak,
but with truth and love to aid you, nothing else.
*

Miracles are not the stuff of fancy, dreams or fable -
they are real.
They don't just happen on grand scale
but in normal daily life,
when intention, time and Earth's raw energy
knit together and join as one against all odds.
Each time we let this happen
a live miracle can occur.

Humanity is the single most powerful force
after Nature and Earth itself.
When your earthly time is through
and you review what flowed from you,
will you consider yourself an asset or a drain?
Utilise this day to become your full potential.

*

God requires man's assistance
to set life's balance straight;
not only for his own sake
but for all that will occur
from this point forward.

*

God is not an entity separate from you.
Nor is it a living power to fear or worship.
Instead God is within you.
God formulates part of you.
Once you realise
God will grant you living proof.

*

I need nothing from you but your conscious connection,
positive energy, compassion, companionship and love. (I am I)

*

Your total life span is your offering to me.
You add to my living life force·and life frame.
I need for you to love this journey
and your life experience
for in doing so you channel these to me. (I am I)

*

I respect man, but does man respect me?
What is said and done to life is equally done unto me.
Earth is my body. It is man's to explore.
Treat it kindly with love and respect. (I am I)

Don't live your life as if treading water,
expecting death to take you on to some place better.
Understand instead; it's life right here that matters most.
It is the garden you were born to know, love and enjoy.

*

Let self-limiting beliefs fall away from you now.
You are not your parents,
your surroundings,
your belongings or your peers.
You are unique
and you are powerful in your own right.

*

This day, this time frame,
can never be repeated or replaced.
Use it well.

*

When blockages threaten to engulf the way ahead,
send healing to punch its way through.
Ask with your thoughts and your needs
will be met wherever possible.

*

When life does not go according to plan,
it possibly just wasn't the right time.
Whether the problem lies with you
or with other people around,
sit tight, remain ready,
and await a new opportunity.

*

You connect with life but you must also give life
time to connect properly with you to assist you.
Patience allows all that's necessary
to fall into place as it should.

All outcomes are open and possible.
Live life as God would intend.

*

At the end of each day, review backwards
all events that occurred.
Be glad for the good,
send healing to the rest,
and know tomorrow is a fresh start.

*

*If you remember your original goal,
notice how far you have come
with me by your side. (I am I)*

*

Life has many sides, facets, levels and links.
All communicate and connect without exception.
Become aware of what you feed it from within.

*

Life needs freedom as much as form and structure.
Allow things around you the freedom to shift and change
before being locked into place.

*

Be careful not to take from the earth more than you really need,
or later what you will need might not be there.

*

Never mind who's right or wrong, blame no one specifically.
Seek out the bottom line,
implement what should be done
and then move on.

*

Why would you think you are not good enough?
You are at one with God even now.

*

The full power of God is with you at this moment.
Have courage and confidence in this fact.

What is it that you want to achieve?
Seek the answer and then live it as reality.

*

You are the beliefs that you live, not your present life status.
Closely monitor your thought content and
notice when you put yourself down.

*

When you live life
as though you are an instrument of God,
you really are.

*

Many want to work with Spirit, with God;
few are chosen.
When you feel that you are called
trust and go with it.

*

Never underestimate the power of God.

*

Use every moment to its fullest potential;
re-defining and enhancing who you are.

*

When life does not meet expectations,
cultivate understanding and patience instead.

*

Become more aware of how you utilise life;
notice what you give and what you take.

*

God will always find ways to enhance you,
but first you must help for this to occur.

Life evolves, things change and shift
through our conscious thinking input on a daily basis.
How fast, how far, how deep, how bad or good
these shifts will be depends entirely
on the subconscious contentment levels displayed.

*

Nobody but you can fulfil your soul agenda.
I will inspire, support, heal and guide.
All I ask is that you remember I exist. (I am I)

*

Decide from this moment that things will be different,
and move in a positive direction.

*

Life must ebb and flow,
so do minutes, hours and days.
What seems appropriate to you now
may alter later on.
Remain confident in your choice
but be aware that the goalposts might shift.

*

Any time you feel unhappy,
come back to base and let things go.
Allow trouble, thoughts and sadness to fall away.
When you're back at inner peace,
let life flow a little more.
Concentrate fully on present tasks
and then move on.

*

Mend friend and family bridges that have broken.
When others don't connect,
send them healing and loving thoughts,
until the past, hurt, and negativity melt away.

Be pleased that you are not at the end of your life journey,
but in the middle where there's ample time
to rethink, grow and change.

*

Let past restrictions fall away.
Today is a brand new chance to re-create.

*

When life will not connect
as you anticipate or need,
the fault may lie with others,
not with you.
Send healing, love and light to repair the situation
and be ready to try again at a later date.

*

Not everything can wait until a time that you are ready.
If something calls for action, then respond.

*

When something is out of order
life will always let you know.
The trick is to know how best to change it.

*

Humanity will experience many lifetimes upon Earth,
and each will be the most important yet.
Together we combine, to evolve and take life forward.
The future is being born through each of us. (I am I)

*

Divine interactions happen daily,
often without acknowledgement or thanks.
This is not miraculously fantastic
but a natural part of life.
Today be consciously aware when this occurs.

*

When you find your inner peace, you link with me. (I am I)

When you're unsure of what to do or say, do nothing,
then act according to the laws of truth and kindness.

*

No effort will ever be wasted.

*

If you only knew the unseen help that's working with you daily
you would not feel alone or without life purpose ever again.

*

I walk with you, but do you walk with me? (I am I)

*

To work with me is not difficult; just be you. Be who you are.
Be true to your highest self and best intentions. (I am I)

*

Enough fear and darkness exists in this life.
Be pleased you can live in the light.

*

If you feel doubt, look further afield.
Once you find the relevant answers,
act according to that knowledge.
If there is no ground for what you feel,
recycle your inner turmoil and return to peace.

*

When I am your first port of call, all things are possible. (I am I)

*

Feed wisdom to your hungry mind.
Not gossip, hype or fiction,
for you are living what you think and believe.

*

When you look for flaws in life and in others,
you'll find them.
When you keep an open mind and look for better things
you'll find those too,
so the outcome of today is up to you.

Allow blame and righteousness to fall away,
in case it might one day bounce back and bite you.
Bring your life force back to peace and then move on.

*

Your forefathers give their blessings and their love.
Remember as you live that you still connect with them
so now continue on, according to that knowledge.

*

All occurrences on earth are known and recognised in Spirit.
Nothing is hidden, all is heard,
so be wise in the actions you take.

*

We each have a live energy store cupboard
that empties or fills according to life deeds and karma.
Be aware of the knock-on effect of what you personally generate.

*

How can we measure the life purpose and value of another
when all people are equal and important
to the web of Earth's consciousness and life?

*

What you think, you actualise and become.

*

There is no order of greatness between human beings.
All are the same. All are here now for a reason.
All are linked into the oneness of life.
All are just facets of the whole.

*

The past is over; don't relive it and waste today in its wake.

*

If you don't receive your just rewards in this physical life
you will definitely reap them in another,
for this is life's cause and effect.

Not all of your efforts will be recognised by others.
But your life's blueprint, your soul will retain and compute
forever what you've done with your life force.

*

Pay attention to detail. Let nothing important be missed.

*

You may know all you are and all you have been,
but I know exactly the all that you can be. (I am I)

*

You are the best you can be at this time. (I am I)

*

As above, in the Kingdom of Heaven,
it should be also in the Kingdom of Earth.

*

When times are tough, conserve your strength.
Tread water until life can flow freely.

*

Not everyone will understand what you know.
Allow them the freedom to grow and move forward
at their own pace, but send them healing,
love and light in the meantime.

*

Life is simple. Don't make it harder than it need be. (I am I)

*

Look beyond what is immediately apparent.

*

When all is said and done, this is your life,
your real-time soul journey.
Live and enjoy all you can.

*

When you think, walk, talk and live a meaningful life,
radiance and light emanate from within,
to touch and embrace all around.

What is it you need
that has not been provided or freely given?
In the end you are just what you are.

*

Love family, friends and strangers to your greatest ability.
See everyone as an extension of yourself.

*

When you peel away all facets of your personality and ego,
you will find your inner radiance and vital essence.
Sit within that space and know yourself.

*

To live as if in wakeful sleep
is to lose power and potential that could be great.
Ensure you remain fully present and alert.

*

It looks darkest before the dawning of the next stage.

*

Things are not always as we expect them to be.
Don't prejudice the experience ahead.

*

You are manifesting only through divine intent.

*

No one sets out to harm or cause you pain.
Allow everything to come back to peace
and start again from a less challenging perspective.

*

No one but you can feel the weight you bear.
Close your eyes.
Put down your load, so it may be dealt with
one step at a time.

*

Awareness is born from knowing, experience and understanding.

Help one another. Be patient and kind.
Each day that passes can never be relived again.

*

Remain positive and stay on course.
Don't let anything pull you off track.

*

You have no one to impress but yourself and your Creator.

*

Don't stop believing; the best is about to come through.

*

Find your highest truth and fly with it.

*

You are an extension of God,
of all things infinite and divine.
Live life accordingly, now.

*

One love - one life - we all are connected.

*

You are worth more than you realise. (I am I)

*

What many see as real is just illusion. Go within.
Find your own truth and work with it now.

*

Trust.

*

Measure your success by those who know and love you;
not through possession, wealth and gain.

*

Remain wholly in the moment,
so that the moment can utilise your strengths and talents
whenever necessary.

If you want to be of service,
if you want to make a difference,
then be as God would intend.
Make that your reality check.

*

When you are completely transparent
you've nothing to hide;
you're living your truth now and always.

*

For inspiration and understanding to filter through,
let go of busy thoughts and specific outcome.
An empty mind space is what is called for at this time.

*

Miracles occur when time, energy, spirit and intent are as one.
Be focused, be open, and be aware.

*

Let go of the reins you've been holding so tight
so that love, life and change can flow with you.

*

The way is blocked. Remain still for until the time it clears. (I am I)

*

*Never underestimate my potential
to step in to give you help whenever necessary. (I am I)*

*

Will you hear me when I call you? (I am I)

*

You need life to play its part to help you,
so move slowly and let things catch up.

*

Focus fully on now, for here lies the power of life.

*

Past mistakes are really just that. Let them go.
Don't waste the power of today
reliving what cannot be changed.

Return to me with your whole mind and soul.
Trust, and I can carry you forward. (I am I)

*

All you need is forthcoming.
Change nothing in this present time frame.

*

Time is but an illusion.
Step out of the box and view what you know
from an unattached angle.

*

Life needs you, just as you need it.
Pick up your potential and work with it

*

The future is not written
but made manifest from activities of now.
What will you will life to be?

*

Let go. You are pushing too hard.
Allow room for intervention and movement.

*

Will you be willing to help me? (I am I)

*

To end the cycles of karma and re-birth,
wake up and be aware of your soul.
Work through your whole life from that viewpoint.

*

I am with you even now. (I am I)

*

Life is easy, not difficult.
Return to the basics and live from the perspective of now.

*

Errors are simply bad choices or deeds.
Don't repeat them. Move on.

Notice what you do automatically and unnecessarily,
and stop doing it.

*

Everything equates to positive or negative.
Reassess where you are and change your mind focus accordingly.

*

What is your purpose? What is your aim?
What will you achieve by your actions?

*

Sit down. Let everything go.
When you return to an inner state of peace
you will move along better in the direction that you need to go.

*

Visualise the situation with the outcome already achieved.
Now, like a balloon, let it go.
Continue with your day as before.

*

Nothing is permanent, except me.
In the end this will be all that matters.
Worry less and come back to your inner point of peace. (I am I)

*

Talk to me. Let me share your fears and secrets.
I will talk back to you through any means that I can.
Watch, listen, be open, be patient. (I am I)

*

There are no short cuts. All must link in to cause and effect.

*

Don't worry, you will make the right choice
and hit the right buttons for now.

*

I am right at your side; you will not fall.
Keep this day in order and press on. (I am I)

*

You are paving the way for ascension.

Everyone is at their own stage
of development and understanding.
Remember that they are not you.

*

Will you trust me enough to help you?
Step back and let go of the reins.
Allow things to shape and reform. (I am I)

*

Allow me to lead the way.
Let life open up and flow a little more
before you take the next step. (I am I)

*

The Light of the World is working through you. (I am I)

*

Find the inner peace that sits permanently within you
and then work the day from that point. (I am I)

*

You have tried everything that you knew how to do.
Now take a new route with my blessing to aid you. (I am I)

*

Let go of clamouring emotions.
Nothing can harm you; you are safe.
Keep peaceful and small; now reassess.

*

Dragons and danger may appear unexpectedly but,
when you work and walk with me,
no harm can ever really befall you. (I am I)

*

When life fails to go according to plan,
don't despair or add negative emotions.
Instead, understand that life has highs and lows too.
Remain positive and ready for things
to transpose and change pace.

Many are chosen, many respond, but very few learn or excel.
You are one of the few. Walk tall, keep going, be strong.

*

Why think the worst when the best that can be is in reach? (I am I)

*

Despite what you think,
you are in exactly the right place at this time.

*

*When your thoughts are mainly centred on me,
no worry or fear can get in. (I am I)*

*

*With your eyes, ears and mind recognise the live link back to me
in everyone and everything you encounter. (I am I)*

*

*Everything I am I give freely to you.
What is it you give back to me? (I am I)*

*

Dreams remain null and void until they are put into action.

*

Thoughts are instructions to life and the planet,
so watch carefully where you allow yours to roam.

*

*Life is rising. You are too.
Keep on going the way that you are. (I am I)*

*

*What is the purpose of being here on this planet,
if not to love and be happy, to enjoy your life's journey
and to live to life's greatest potential? (I am I)*

*

In life no golden rules or guarantees exist.
Every moment, event, relationship is different.
Let go and experience each fully.

When you understand your attachment
to situations and to people
you can begin to heal and move on.
Everything around you is there for a purpose.
Dig deep, understand and let go.

*

To 'let go' does not mean to throw aside or cast away,
but to loosen your hold, attachment,
influence or grip,
to set free, to no longer require or need
in quite the same way.
To let go might mean only for now.

*

Life is as difficult or easy as you believe it to be.
Focus your energy on the latter,
and let it unfold for you now. (I am I)

*

When the going seems tough,
lay down your task, take a break,
do something different
to disperse or disrupt
the stale energy;
then resume, refreshed and renewed.

*

When you work with me, the impossible becomes the achieved. (I am I)

*

Don't look for me with physical eyes,
for through them I will not be visible.
Instead use your senses, your intuition, your knowing
for I am the all that is everywhere. (I am I)

When your ego feels tattered, let down and torn,
do nothing to respond or retaliate.
When this feels too hard or too painful to bear,
again hold your ground and do nothing.
Instead take deep breaths.
I will help you keep strong,
for when all this has passed
you'll be in the right place,
with the higher hand. (I am I)

*

I trust you with my body and my life;
to live as you should live
and to honour this life journey you are on. (I am I)

*

You are one cog in the whole wheel of life.
If you were to cease or break
so would other things too.
Keep going. Gain momentum.
Don't quit. (I am I)

*

Your efforts are never wasted,
even though they may not seem to bear fruit at this time.

*

Change and rebalance can spark turmoil and fear
before things begin to get better.
Don't be alarmed with shifts that occur.
Remain calm, centred and focused,
and all will be fine once life settles itself once more.

*

Change manifests in many ways,
some large and immediate, some slow and unseen.
It takes the effort of many, just as much as the effort of one.

Surrender all you are, all you have been
and all you can be to me.
I know and love you for all facets of yourself.
Every part you've played
was important in the moulding of you.
Now we can work this together. (I am I)

*

No one can teach you what you will not learn.
You have gained much from the past.
Find and use your strengths well.
Life is calling upon you to work with it,
in a way that you alone can,
to help those who need help on your path.

*

What are you willing your efforts to achieve?
I try to help you gain clarity and direction,
but you must be clear and true with your aim. (I am I)

*

Many words and truths have been written over time.
How many more are yet to come? Who can tell?
The truths they portray will be the same.
You are individual, yet joined to God.
You are unique, yet the same as all of life.
You choose your journey, yet you have a pre-destined life agenda.
You are here for the time that this life time will take,
but you are eternal, immortal and unending.
All you are, you feed to life.
You form part of the life that is all life and
you are responsible for what you bring to it.

*

You have greatness and power to manifest and change.
At all times you can choose from many options.
This is your life to live. Fulfil your potential and use it well.
When it's over, you'll assess how you did.

This day is your own to use as you will.
Enjoy the freedom that this represents. (I am I)
*

Everyone is the same, yet also very different.
Respect both. (I am I)
*

Your soul is your own, yet it connects and works with me.
Good and bad are the choices you choose from.
Every moment you are here, living physically upon earth,
you have the chance to make a difference, to set some balance right.
How you live is what you give. It's your offering back to me.
You feed your life force into my own force,
as a river feeds the sea and vice versa.
What you see everywhere, you also help to create.
Your soul connects to my soul, the all of life. (I am I)
*

Love is the greatest gift we all share.
Not romance but warmth, compassion, understanding,
service, tolerance, listening and patience.
When you operate from this space
all will be as it should in your now.
*

Your ancestors worked hard to give you freedom and choice.
Don't let all that effort be for nothing.
Worry less, smile more, recognise the freedom,
health and liberty that you have.
*

Find the energy you need to get your tasks done.
Push past your personal fatigue.
Put on some music, let in some fresh air,
break free of the cycle you're presently in, and crack on.
*

Work this day to its greatest potential. (I am I)

We trust you to make the world better;
to help make a difference, to give something back,
to live your life journey to the highest standard that you can achieve.
We ask you trust us the same way; to assist, to inspire,
to combine and work with you as one. (I am I)

*

Sometimes you need a little time out. Today is one of those times.

*

Clear your mind of clutter and undue expectation.
Allow me to give you new insight and knowledge
to accomplish what needs to be done. (I am I)

*

The greatest gift you can give me is the gift of your life,
your conscious activity and awareness.
Let me join with you to complete the whole process.
Together we will work to clear mountains. (I am I)

*

Without effort, good intentions are worthless.

*

Nature works on time and in order.
Work your own life in the same way.

*

What you think to be your best I will always take you higher.
For I know your soul's capabilities. (I am I)

*

Not every day will be profound.
The most ordinary, approached in the correct manner,
can attain greatness and be of the most value.
Life needs time to catch up.
You need time to take stock and re-group.
Enjoy this natural lull in activity.

Whatever you worship in this life,
you'll most likely attain in the next.
Worship false gods and idols,
you'll join others who did the same.
When you work and believe solely in me,
you'll attain the highest heights, you'll be home. (I am I)

*

Every form of religion has its own take on truth and on me.
Move beyond what is preached.
I will guide and work with you by my own hand. (I am I)

*

When you hit obstacles, adversity, barriers and fear,
be kind, understanding and gentle.
Use me to send healing to repair and address
what is necessary.
Be patient and all will be well. (I am I)

*

Look around and take stock of those
who love and care for you.
Take pleasure in the fact that they do.

*

All life interlinks. All is as one.
Nothing can separate from the whole.
Every atom that exists belongs to me.
Together we create; we gather knowledge,
meaning and understanding of what life is,
how it feels, how it evolves and moves forward
through time. (I am I)

*

Every day presents opportunities, obstacles and live information
to process and to work with accordingly.
Be aware of what flows to and from you and why.
It is precisely these times that we connect and interact strongly. (I am I)

Notice your thoughts and thought content.
Should negativity arise, let it go quickly, so as not to give it life
through your own mind's energy, focus and life force.

*

Life passes quickly.
Don't put off what can easily be accomplished today.

*

Turn your attention to the important tasks that are waiting.
The remainder you can pick up again later.

*

How are you helping life? Everyone tries,
but not all succeed in the assets they share and complete. (I am I)

*

Nothing is given that you cannot do.
You are capable of more than you realise.

*

When you work and talk with God, everything becomes possible,
for you then link directly with Source.

*

Let go, and let God take the helm on your behalf,
for this day at least.

*

Every living soul remains linked to me,
whether physical upon earth or in Spirit.
What is done to another is done also to me.
Try to act kindly, with compassion
and respect at all times. (I am I)

*

Cause and effect are the balance keepers of life.
Nothing remains hidden or unseen.
Your best effort to keep life in good order
will prevent things bouncing back later on.

No one but you can make your life work.
Your effort is required to turn the wheels to win through. (I am I)
*

Inspiration is available on tap. You only need ask and it is yours.
*

Will you hear when you are called
to contribute the life assets that you have?
*

The smallest step in the right direction at the right time joins to
others; together they will accomplish great feats.
*

In the beginning there was the light and word of God.
Now life is channelled by man, who wields and distributes
Earth's raw creative force through his live interaction upon it.
Understand what you are asking to occur.
*

Each time you smile you send out love and live positive energy.
You literally add light to the world where you go.
*

Remember you came here to assist others home,
to know your own self and to help your soul grow.
What you achieve here stays with you beyond physical life,
so take time to fine tune what you can.
*

Time is irrelevant, for there exists only now.
Now is where life's full power lies.
*

If you do nothing, nothing happens. I will help you in any way that is
necessary, but you too must play your part in that process. (I am I)

When you are asked to do something
that throws you out of sync - don't moan -
get it done and let it go.
Interruptions have their own part to play.
Every task means something somewhere is finished.

*

People grow at their own rate and pace.
Knowledge you hold might be greater than those around you.
Today be ready to share what is needed.

*

Many words have been spoken throughout the ages of time.
Understanding still needs to filter through.

*

Life only needs assistance when bumps occur or changes happen.
Until then, let things roll as they are.

*

Don't get tied up by events that can't be changed.
Do what's right. Keep things calm and move on.

*

Do your best and let others do the same.

*

Never lose sight of what truth shaped your goal,
for only there will you find what you need
to keep going and win.

*

Remember that you never work alone.
Let go and let knowing pour in.

*

Don't rely on your emotions because they change.
Find the truth of the bottom line and go with that.

*

Let go of your fears and come back to peace,
nothing is the way that you think.
When your thoughts have calmed down, look again.

Like comes to like.
To receive the best keep your own channels
clear and guilt free.
You have the rest of your life to fine tune your game.
I will help you, but you must also help me. (I am I)

*

You may think you are back at square one, but you're not.
Things are different this time, you have grown, and you have
experience, knowledge, strength and love to draw from.
Keep calmly balanced, remain small and move on.

*

Why are you here? What is your life trying to show you?
What weaknesses pull you down or hold you back?
What strengths help you forward?
What does your soul need to achieve?

*

I can go ahead to smooth the path if you let me,
but first you must be clear with what you need. (I am I)

*

Don't be rigid in your outlook or your thoughts.
Keep all options open and be aware of what it is that you need.

*

What do you need from today?
How may you serve?
How may you be assisted yourself?
When others around you are struggling for help,
send out silent request signals to me. (I am I)

*

Don't rush in before life is in place to assist you.

I am the beginning, the middle and the end
that will never end - for I am eternal.
Humanity forms part of me.
All that I am, so is mankind too.
Man and Earth are one, and all is me. (I am I)

*

Nothing can be gained without effort.

*

You achieve not only for the self but for life eternal.
Through your efforts you show others the way.

*

You are not segregated or separate,
but joined and interacting with life.

*

Love and light are the true driving factors in the world.

*

Understanding, respect, hard work, devotion, willingness to
listen, to learn and remember are facets of the very same things.

*

Don't doubt my ability to step up to the mark
to provide help and guidance when asked.
I don't doubt you,
despite what you have done in the past. (I am I)

*

We will work with you to get life on track,
to turn around what is necessary. (I am I)

*

Man is powerful within his own right.
But joined correctly in mind force with me,
he becomes a force greater than I. (I am I)

*

Truth will always win through.

*

You are the eyes, ears and thinking mind of life now. (I am I)

Life needs you to step up to the mark.
Live the journey you came to complete
and waste it no more. (I am I)

*

It will not be necessary to repeat this again
once you wake up and hit the right buttons.
You will be able to move on
to the next phase awaits you. (I am I)

*

You came here to punch through the blockages of life.
So begin, not through force but through persistence, love,
knowledge and the understanding that life follows on.

*

Heaven is not myth, but fact.
It exists here and now;
it is the next phase of mankind's existence.
You have been there before and will do so again,
once your physical time on this planet is through.
Use the rest of this time to achieve
what you wish to take with you.

*

Please become aware of what is being done to me.
Earth is my body.
It provides all that you need;
it offers protection, sustenance
and somewhere to live.
Without it you could not be here. (I am I)

*

Instead of taking, give back.

*

Don't judge. Understand what you see
then ask for the opposite, for those in need, to come in.
I will adjust what I can in any way that is open to help. (I am I)

Let go of the thoughts of things that you can't change.
Instead work on those that you can.

*

To help does not mean to interfere or take on board
what is not yours to carry or complete.
Instead use your thoughts.
Ask me to step in to do what is needed and necessary. (I am I)

*

Many are called into service,
but not all respond or complete their task,
will you be someone who does? (I am I)

*

Who said that you will not achieve what you set out to do?
When it comes from the heart, when it's part of your journey,
it will happen. (I am I)

*

Clean and clear up your life and your mind space.
Only then will you see the next step. (I am I)

*

I hear your thoughts.
I know you. (I am I)

*

Only you can fix what needs fixing.
Begin with your internal self.

*

Miracles are not impossible. Keep going. (I am I)

*

Get real, let go of illusion.
Focus your thoughts on where you are now.
Take small steps and build up from this point. (I am I)

*

Take small steps. Don't make waves.
When what is needed appears,
take it steady and all will be well. (I am I)

It is not a fluke that you are where you are. Enjoy it. (I am I)

*

For inspiration to flow freely you must let attachment fall away. (I am I)

*

You are not the first to follow this path
and you surely will not be the last.
Ensure that you use your time well.

*

Others might not understand, but you do.
You have had an awakening, a life-changing experience.
Don't allow yourself to be pulled off track.

*

You have turned much around but there is more to come.
Hold tight and let life shift around you.
This process will not harm you in any way.

*

Thoughts are loud and clear within the realms of Spirit.
Spoken word is physical and is used only here on earth.
Take heed of what you freely generate. (I am I)

*

This is a time of enlightenment and growth.
You chose to be part of that process. (I am I)

*

When you have a quiet moment think of the link you share with me,
for I need your interaction and your love. (I am I)

*

You trust in me and for this I thank you. For this I am able to guide and
help you. I can shield you and soften life's storms. (I am I)

*

You are loved. You are known, understood and recognised
for what has driven and shaped you through life.
Let go and become all that you should be. (I am I)

*

For the rest of your days follow your insights and grow.

One life, one Earth, one Universe.

*

Every life, every soul, is precious to me.
I need you to value yourself.
Not in the mirror
but through deeds and the days yet to come. (I am I)

*

What is the price of a life?
What value is placed upon Earth?
Yet its assets are freely available
for mankind to use through free will.

*

Each living soul will work within
the window of knowledge that it has attained.
What it gains by experience
will take it much nearer to God.

*

Feel the power that courses through you,
even as you read these words.
This is proof that we link and work and live as one. (I am I)

*

It is necessary to be neutral at this time.

*

Pick up your strengths and life calling for the sake of Heaven,
for God and world peace.

*

All energy that you generate, both good and bad,
will filter again back to you.

*

Signs and signals do come forth from many places,
but not at this time.
Come back to a state of inner peace.

*

I fulfil the wishes of man. I trust man to honour mine too. (I am I)

Life is fragile. It needs balance and consideration.
Take nothing for granted. (I am I)

*

There will always be those who disturb the peace,
who are yet to wake up, who believe only in that which they see.
You are not them. You have your own mind and knowledge.
Do what you know to be right. (I am I)

*

Each moment teams with its own potency and power.
Nothing is written in stone. All outcomes are possible.
Focus on the things that require your attention.
Be mindful of what you wilfully generate.

*

This window in time is fleeting. Enjoy it.

*

Work from the heart. Worry not.
Keep your wishes within focus and keep going.

*

No one is better than you.

*

What is the best outcome for you at this time?
What needs to change? What processes must happen to get there?
Not all problems are yours to carry or solve.
Help where you can or where it's appropriate
and pass the rest over to me. (I am I)

*

When you pass things over to me,
I can help from behind the main scene. I can work from within. (I am I)

*

You are at life's helm. Take control so others can then follow you.
(I am I)

Wisdom is born from knowledge, experience and understanding.
You have worked hard to get to this point.
Trust and all will be well. (I am I)

*

Don't quit. Live connections are not far away.

*

Why live with the worst,
when the best is waiting to come in?
Every moment will count.

*

Every word has its place.
Make sure you say what is needed.
How can life connect with you
if you don't connect with it?
Step out from the shadows
and work with the talents you have.

*

Do not rehearse what you think should be said.
Instead allow things to flow as they will
at the time conversation is shared.

*

When life does not flow as you think it should,
step back and return to inner peace.
Concentrate fully on the moment at hand
and allow time a little more room.

*

Repetition equates to stability at this time.
It adds substance to the backbone of life.

*

The most ordinary can be the most powerful.
Keep things simple.

Where you see only empty space, I am there.
Where you see only separate objects,
they connect and join through me.
Where you see life fragmented, all is linked.
I am all life, all things everywhere connected. (I am I)

*

You know that I exist, that I'm real.
I've proven it through the ages many times. (I am I)

*

Believe.

*

When all seems lost, don't lose yourself.
This experience will soon exist behind you,
so keep strong. (I am I).

*

Your best effort is always enough.

*

Let unnecessary thoughts and old patterns fall away
as new ones need to come in,
to help you and to aid your time management.

*

I need you and your real-time life force.
When life is tough, keep all links with me clear and open.
that I may aid you in ways that are possible. (I am I)

*

Life will not harm you. I will not leave.
Live to your greatest potential. (I am I)

*

There is always another choice.
Find it with the time that is spare. (I am I)

*

Not everything is available immediately on tap.
Time needs to interact too.

You have nothing to prove.
Let go of anxiety, fear, apprehension, stress and worry.
The next step will present itself soon. (I am I)
*

Come back to the central point of your own inner being.
Let go of the script that you are living by now.
Don't buy into another's illusion.
*

Your base requirements are already being met.
All else is surplus.
Find your inner state of peace that sits within.
*

Life knows nothing beyond that which it is.
Man gives it labels and meaning.
Step back and enjoy all it is.
*

Let limiting thoughts and ego fall away.
Nothing is present here to hurt or harm you.
*

Live your truth. Be the light that others may see and then follow.
*

Patience is difficult, but crucial.
*

There is no past or present,
only one continuous, unending, unfolding now.
*

You are not the same as others before;
don't repeat the same actions.
Take note of all sides and cover the middle ground instead.
Do what is best for you now. (I am I)
*

If you don't live your truth, then who will?

Rely on your own self as well as me.
That is where your true power lies. (I am I)

*

You are wide awake and are working with me,
but others are not.
Focus on what needs your thought and attention. (I am I)

*

Take a break, life needs to catch up,
not everything is yet in place the way it should be.

*

Words are not good here. Trust your instinct.

*

The doubts and fears of what's ahead,
you have placed there as an obstacle.
Nothing can cause you harm,
so pass the whole matter to me to recycle.
From this moment on remain positive and blank.
Allow things to unfold in the way that they will.
I will help where I can, when you let me. (I am I)

*

What will you achieve with your now?

*

Yesterday, tomorrow and today in reality have no meaning.
All blend together as now.

*

Life will always let you know when it requires assistance.

*

You are incredible for all you have done and endured,
for perfecting what you have become.
Others around might not know or understand,
but I do. (I am I)

*

Intention is nothing without action.

Love emanates from the soul. (I am I)

*

When you understand, you do not judge or condemn.
When you love and forgive, you will not hate and compound the subject.
These replacement attitudes link directly with me. (I am I)

*

You will not fall; just keep going. (I am I)

*

Feelings are linked to emotions.
Both are liable to alter and change. At this time trust neither.
Come back to the safety of your inner point of peace and be still.

*

When you are at peace, when you live your truth,
life will shift and change around you. (I am I)

*

Only unconditional love will take you
to your next level of growth and fulfilment

*

Contain and recycle all frustrations and anger.
Don't add to the problem. Step back so that light can step in.
You will be able to share your truth later on. (I am I)

*

What is it that you need from me? (I am I)

*

Don't doubt.

*

Everyone is on a journey that will aid or detract from their soul.
Cause and effect will always interplay,
so don't judge what you hear, see or feel.

*

When you work with me, time has not the same pull as before.
You have the rest of your life to perfect and fine tune.
Don't rush. Nothing can be born before its time. (I am I)

Every day is important.
However, don't forget about yourself in the process.

*

You are an extension of me and my life-giving energy force.
I have given you free will to work with and to use as is necessary.
(I am I)

*

What will be gained from this action?

*

True love is not forceful. It is understanding, patient and kind.
Let go and allow things to settle.

*

Listen and be there for someone who needs you,
but don't take on board as yours
what they need to complete for themselves.

*

Finish one task at a time. Yes.

*

While you rest I will work on your behalf
to put things in place for all concerned. (I am I)

*

Everything is born from imagination.

*

Let me work with you. (I am I)

*

I place my trust in your ability to do the right thing. (I am I)

*

People have agendas that might not work in sync with your own.
Remain flexible in what you need to accomplish

*

Much of each day will be spent on the mundane and normal.

*

This is fine. You will know when I need your help and assistance.
(I am I)

Forget what you thought before this point in time.
There is a new way to approach this. (I am I)

*

You will achieve all you need to, but take one small step at a time.

*

Only you have the vision to make this project work.
Rely on no other but yourself.

*

With the Light of the World, walk in peace.

*

. Through me you have the full force of creation to work with.
Realise this. Realise the power you own.
Work always towards the highest good and potential,
for it is there that I am with you. (I am I)

*

Bend like the willow.
Don't take interruptions as detrimental.
A short break may let a new approach filter through.

*

You don't yet realise how far you have come,
how important and unique you are.
Many embark on this journey, but many again turn away.
You have not. You are still strong.
You are forging a path for more who are like you to follow. (I am I)

*

From the soul's point of view love renders us complete,
that's why we continuously yearn for it.

*

Believe in your abilities
so the power of your mind can win through.

*

Every thought and feeling has a subsequent reaction on your
body. The choice of whether this is positive or negative is up
to you.

You think you cannot save the world, yet you can.
When you work in sync with me it only takes a few to lift the vibration
and intelligence of many.
Trust in me as I trust in you. (I am I)

*

This day and its experience, you have not had before.
So let it play out and be all it will be without pre-conception.

*

Why is your life getting better? Is it by your own hand alone?
Or by your interactions with me? (I am I)

*

Time has no bearing on matters of the soul.
Growth and progress have no limits or boundaries.
Yet the urgency you feel is compelling you on.
So go with it, as your calling dictates. (I am I)

*

Life is a journey of soul growth and progression.
Notice the pattern you weave and what you'll take with you
as gains and triumphs from the time your soul has spent here.

*

I am the Light and the Truth.
Your ego tries to shield you from what it fears, yet you are safe.
You have the power to decide which route to follow. (I am I)

*

Time is irrelevant.
It simply places life into usable working sectors,
to mould and apply what is chosen or necessary,
to aid and enhance here and now.

*

Many times have you been here before.
What now is important will shift and change.
Take time to understand and enjoy this experience
while it occurs in this segment of now.

What can I give that has not already been given?
What do you need to be happy? (I am I)

*

Nothing you perceive has meaning beyond that
which you or another will give it.
Step aside and reassess the situation and
what it is that you think should be happening.

*

Work not on your body and lifestyle,
but on your awareness and understanding instead.

*

Whatever it is that you think you can achieve,
I will take you higher, beyond what you now perceive as your best.
Don't worry when life does not flow as you expect.
The old must fall away for the new. (I am I)

*

Work to find inner peace.
The future is shaped with all you are now,
by the ideas and thoughts you give life to.

*

When you work with me, every day will be balanced and calm.
Nothing will ruffle your feathers.
If it does, let it go, return to peace. (I am I)

*

You carry my life force within you. (I am I)

*

My life does not depend wholly on yours,
but your wellbeing depends entirely on mine.
I entrust you to understand and work with this. (I am I)

*

Neither vague nor obscure, but powerful and overwhelming,
enlightenment and revelation will dawn.

Every step you take on the journey of self-progression
will benefit the consciousness of all
and actively raise the vibration of many. (I am I)
*

Let go, so knowingness can flow through.
*

Let perceptions fall away. I know what you need, so let go.
Focus on current tasks, add nothing more,
and allow time and other influences to help. (I am I)
*

Fear, hatred, anger, revenge, resentment and spite
are all self-indulgent perceptions of loss or pain.
Come back to inner peace;
pass these feelings up to me to recycle
and to aid whatever's next. (I am I)
*

Await the next truth to appear.
*

Operate always from the position of recognition,
understanding, compassion and soul to soul love.
No higher perspective exists.
*

Don't look to others to supply what you want or need.
All is already within your own reach.
When life appears heavy, don't quit.
Talk to me, for I know what you need and also why. (I am I).
*

Love underpins everything that is known
in the physical and spiritual world. (I am I)
*

New ways are opening up.
Patience is necessary.

The choice to grow was made by you long ago.
The time is now, but how far and how fast
is driven by your present intention.

*

Why are you walking this path?
Remember the reasons you chose to wake up
and make the most of opportunities accordingly (I am I)

*

Let go of personal attachment and thoughts of loss or gain.
Impartiality and observation are crucial here. (I am I)

*

Polarities of wrong or right, bad or good,
past or future, gain or loss, yours or mine,
are all illusionary perspectives of now.
Only the truth of the present carries has meaning in reality.

*

Your pain is not personal and linked to you alone.
Instead, it is a living symptom of greater life.
The problem is not that you feel it,
but that you keep it locked inside,
to grow, misshape and fester
until you don't know what to do with it anymore.
I need you to let it go.
In your mind turn it over to me,
in any way or thinking format that you can.
As quickly as you are able, return again to inner peace,
and focus on the moment of your now. (I am I)

*

Even the smallest negative thought
can bounce back and may in turn bite you.

What you see as someone's failure
is the journey of their own soul playing out.
Within your mind pass onto me what needs
assistance or intervention,
as frequently as is necessary or as you wish. (I am I)

*

No one is responsible for how you react to life.
You have the key to your awareness in your own hand.

*

Don't crowd another's space, just work quietly from your own
so that calmness and peace may return. (I am I)

*

Unconditional means exactly that. Let go of everything else.

*

In the scheme of greater life nothing is overlooked,
but sometimes a helping hand will be a Godsend.
As the eyes and ears of now you are a conscious living trigger
to instigate what may be necessary as it appears,
not always by your own hand, but of mine. (I am I)

*

Now.

*

You may feel small and helpless, but you're not.
You connect to the web of life where
even the slightest ripple
links back to the greater whole.
When you think, your thoughts are heard
and I am there. (I am I)

*

Rise higher and stay out of harm's reach.
Don't think - just be.

To work with me is not delusional.
You don't give away your power or close your eyes to life,
but instead the very opposite is true.
You have your eyes wide open, you see and live the truth,
you harness your power with mine, and then direct it. (I am I)

*

Work from the perspective of innocence, understanding and love.
Judge nothing, notice all. (I am I)

*

Honour the responsibilities that belong to you.

*

Live as a light that others may notice and follow.
The best that you can do is good enough. (I am I)

*

If both sides wish to win, the best that I can do is balance out. (I am I)

*

What is your aim? Win through by letting go, not pushing
forward.

*

When you give only love, only love will come to you.
Make sure you keep your mind space clutter free. (I am I)

*

People are different; all will wake up some time.
You are one of a few that are working to help us wake many.

*

Let go of right or wrong. Instead, work with what is.

*

Feel the strength of the connection that we share. (I am I)

*

Wisdom is the property of all, without exception.
Try to help as you've been helped when help is called for.

*

Yesterday is done, don't drag it forward.

Thoughts direct intention and raw creative force.
What you perceive as reality might differ for someone else.
Don't add force, add love. (I am I)

*

Belief is not vital; proof is everywhere.

*

Not everyone will understand where you're at or coming from.
Don't push or try to change, but pull back instead.
Wait for a better opportunity to open up.

*

Nothing is broken.
Check your perspective instead.

*

Let go, and let God work as necessary.

*

Mood swings affect everyone.
Find your personal inner peace,
ask that all else be recycled and move on. (I am I)

*

I will never let you down. (I am I)

*

Everything is perfect at this time,
lessons are being learnt and obstacles transcended;
let all that is occurring settle naturally.

*

Impatience can take you forward too far, too fast.
Differentiate between wants and needs.

*

Push away any thoughts that are unlike your usual pattern,
for these are ego based and will not help.
You may be also picking up what another is dragging with them.
Recognise what does not fit and request recycling. (I am I)

The energy of your soul is getting finer, for it is ascending;
you are working in the light and easing in
the transformation of higher frequencies. (I am I)

*

Not all will have to know the ins and outs of spiritual truths.
Many will simply regain inner peace.

*

The idea is not to become God but to open your life up
to happiness and peace so the pure energy of Earth's own life force
can follow through. (I am I)

*

You are a human being, not a saint.
You came here to explore, not to stagnate.
Enjoy what life presents as the fruits of what you've earned.
Don't label as superficial what in reality should simply
be enjoyed.

*

What you need will come to you. Assume nothing.

*

Follow your intuition, go with what feels right.
Worry not what others think as they are not you.

*

Not everyone on earth works for the greatest good.
Many have beliefs that will serve to hinder. Recognise these occasions.
To speak your truth or to turn away is your own choice -
but at all times call on me to bring in light. (I am I)

*

Every soul has come to earth for different reasons,
so who and where they are should not be measured or condemned.
Karma will keep these matters within order. (I am I)

At all times you are connected with life's greater intelligent
source, but you have discernment, so choose what you take on
board. We are all the same yet innately different so we grow
at different speeds and different levels.
We our present life time to perfect ourselves and grow,
but for all intents and purposes, the time is now.

*

When you can get away with nothing
you are living instant karma.
Be pleased instead of mad, for in this way
you keep your soul space clear and bright.

*

You control your speed of learning at all times, without exception.

*

No need to turn your back on what
you love and hold most dear.
Life does not expect it and there is no need for anything rash.
Instead, return to inner peace and a state of love.

*

What is there to forgive when you now have understanding?
Let go of what has past and then move on.

*

*The love you crave is just obscured
by the natural stress and strain of daily life.
Doubt not its presence. (I am I)*

*

*The future is malleable like plastic.
It can change and shift shape. (I am I)*

*

What use is learning without it being put to action?
Live your truth.

All souls gravitate to the energetic density
of their learning and achievement.
You will attract from life exactly what you need.

*

Remain neutral wherever you can
so as not to add undue force to what's occurring.

*

Wait for the next step to materialise.
Much has been gained by hard work and effort.
Don't rush and spoil what will be. (I am I)

*

Steer clear of negative influence and hearsay.
What you give to your mind you also give back to life.
What you think, you believe, you live; and so you are. (I am I)

*

Every act and every kindness made for the right reasons is
counted and recognised. It adds to your soul and your energy
blueprint, to graduate your assent back to God.

*

Hell and Heaven are choices present in every moment that exists.
You choose which one you will experience
through your view point of your reality,
your internal sense of self that drives perception.
The more neutral you can be the more perception falls away,
the more you can work with life without undue distortion. (I am I)

*

When experienced properly, only now exists.
Past and future have no power or hold. Time itself will seem to stop.
When this occurs you are working with the live creative source.
All that will be stems directly from this point. (I am I)

*

Why do you doubt your ability?
When you mistrust yourself, even just a bit,
you essentially doubt the living life force working through you. (I am I)

Anger, frustration and thoughts of revenge have no part in your life.
When others fail to see what you aim to accomplish,
send peace and love to fill their mind space instead. (I am I)

*

Your inner sense of your reality stems from your life perception.
You react and interact to things around you
through emotions, thoughts, beliefs and feelings that you carry.
Come back to inner peace and look again.

*

When you choose to be at one with joy and peace and God,
nothing will ever occur that you cannot transcend.

*

Step away from past conditioning, from pre-conception
and how society usually states you should respond.
You are your own person; you create your own life story.
Take time out to be kind and honest with yourself. (I am I)
Place trust and faith in the love of God which is all forgiving.
To know your own limitations
is not weakness but strength.
You will not fail.
A willingly relinquished lesser,
always makes way for the greater.

*

Don't be disheartened - keep going.

*

All higher conscious and subconscious acts
add to the greater conscious movement of the whole.
Every act of kindness, every loving compassionate thought
counter-balances the effect of negativity somewhere.
In this manner how you live serves the world.

*

Will the highest outcome at all times.

A small percentage of the population living in the light
positively lifts the energy signature of the whole.

*

No person is too small,
too tall, too thin, too fat,
too poor, too rich,
too stupid, too educated,
to make a difference.

*

Higher levels of thought
are immensely more powerful
than lower negative ones.

*

You are of service to the world,
a vehicle of divine love
and a channel of God's will.
Love and peace must be your options above all else.

*

Surrender any thoughts of negativity and judgement
up to God to be recycled. Return to peace.

*

*You are working with the higher forces of light and love.
Be prepared to send these vibrations where-ever necessary. (I am I).*

*

With understanding - to forgive - becomes irrelevant.

*

*You know what must be done - but life itself must be able to assist.
I wait along with you - for life to show the signs
and signal that all is ready. (I am I).*

*

*If intuition tells you something is not right, listen.
Check things out and move with caution.
Remain wary of moving forward too slow or too quickly. (I am I)*

Every increase in ordinary consciousness effectively lifts the
consciousness of all mankind.

*

Non-action has immense power
in the height of adversity and stress. (I am I)

*

Who knows you better than I do? (I am I)

*

You cannot set the pace that is necessary.
Tread water and be ready for when things change. (I am I)

*

Not all that comes your way is of your making.
Allow what is unproductive to fall away. (I am I)

*

Don't think of the possibility of failure,
but instead the likelihood of success.

*

No event is completely predestined.
Instead, it remains possible to be changed
until actioned through freedom of will. (I am I)

*

Today is a day for hard work.
Let your efforts work in line with your intention. (I am I)

*

How can you trust
when you wait for the worst to appear? (I am I)

*

Why?

*

You are sowing the seeds and clearing the path,
not creating and producing the whole harvest. (I am I)

*

Put aside misconceptions and pick up the challenge. (I am I)

Every moment you change, that very action
changes every other action. (I am I)
*

Many probabilities exist.
How, what, where and when are the choices
that will determine the outcome. (I am I)
*

No one can tell you what road to follow.
You have the answers you need within you. (I am I)
*

You constantly transform your thoughts and emotions
into dense matter and physical form. (I am I)
*

You help shape reality through many lifetimes.
This is the point of your existence and journey. (I am I)
*

When you don't understand where you are being led,
don't put on the brakes.
Trust instead. I will not let go of you now. (I am I)
*

When you raise the barriers of learning and experience,
you move up into new levels of existence. (I am I)
*

It does not fall to you to completely change the world.
Just do your bit, do your best and the rest will come. (I am I)
*

Place your intention with me and watch it unfold in due time. (I am I)
*

When life needs you to slow down to catch up,
nothing will go quite as you think.
The opposite occurs too at times necessary. (I am I)
*

What do you want to occur?

Nothing can remain the same always.
Life must shift and change, and so must you. (I am I)
*

Are your present requirements not being met?
*

Work from the baseline of your own life. (I am I)
*

When the day is mundane, without worry or ripple,
be pleased and send thanks to upstairs. (I am I)
*

Remember to send healing to those around you who need it
whether physical, mental or soul based. (I am I)
*

Want nothing. (I am I)
*

Remove your worry head and replace it with appreciation
instead. Throughout the days that will follow review everything
you encounter from this perspective, as thoughts of appreciation
flow everywhere, nothing else can then enter your mind space.
*

You have worked hard to get to this point.
Well done. (I am I)
*

Where will life take you next?
Don't be too rigid in your routine expectations.
Let the old fall away for the new. (I am I)
*

You will be pleased when you look back
at what has been accomplished by your deeds. (I am I)
*

Remember you live only one part of life.
Others will connect in their own way. (I am I)

I can pre-empt what will be and what is necessary.
So trust that I will not steer you wrong. (I am I)

*

Wait and see. You will be pleased. (I am I)

*

Prayer is conversation delivered in thought form.
I converse back through intuition and
your thoughts between thoughts. (I am I)

*

Close your eyes, return to the light, now carry on. (I am I)

*

Remember you have been here before.
Notice patterns you adhere to,
and then choose to refine what is necessary. (I am I)

*

You have wisdom beyond what you presently realise.
I will help it flow in. (I am I)

*

This phase will pass. (I am I)

*

No other force can help you at this time.
Come back to your own intuition.

*

When you work with me above anything else,
together we shall change the world. (I am I)

*

I hear every thought in your mind. (I am I)

*

Bring in the white light as much as you can
to pierce through the blockages of lethargy. (I am I)

*

How would you feel if your wishes came true?
Today live and breathe as though they have. (I am I)

I have to tell you that you are loved
by more people than you realise. (I am I)
*

Miracles occur all the time.
Each time you notice,
give thanks with your heart and your mind.
Let recognition flow back to life. (I am I)
*

When you think of me morning, noon and night,
when I am your first option always,
nothing will pull you off course. (I am I)
*

Your life revolves around blessings.
Like a child, find and list them,
for as you keep them in focus
more will follow. (I am I)
*

Always talk with me first, regardless of topic,
that I might know what you need
and help you reach it. (I am I)
*

Where you understand the bigger truth
the rest will fall into place.
*

Forgive.
*

Place your worries with me to be dealt with on your behalf. (I am I)
*

Every soul is connected with me,
but not every soul realises or lives to the very best that could be.
Disregard what you might think
and ask me to refresh all connections. (I am I)

Everything must change at some point in time.
Move slowly, with caution and precision.

*

First you must become your best effort.

*

What is the purpose, if not for development and growth? (I am I)

*

Vendettas and grudges serve no one.
Let go and move forward with peace.

*

You cannot always know what is causing the problem,
but to resolve it you have to let go.
I will take over matters on your behalf. (I am I)

*

When things keep repeating, you must look again.
You are missing what needs to be changed. (I am I)

*

Seasons come and go.
So too will these things that you're facing.

*

You have nothing to prove and nothing to lose.
The world is your own to interpret, love and use.
Enjoy the energy you own. (I am I)

*

When you work with me you feel peace and love.
When you let this link close you feel stress. (I am I)

*

What you fail to correct you take with you to Spirit,
so let go of bad habits here and now. (I am I)

*

Never look back with regret.
Stand tall in your now and live as you would like to go on. (I am I)

Who knows the future for sure when it's subject to free will,
outside influence and change?

*

From this point forward you really have nothing to fear.
I trust you to choose what is best at this time. (I am I)

*

You trust me so let me help you move forward.
Let go of the reins so I can help. (I am I)

*

When you look for the answer in too many places you'll only
achieve more confusion.

*

I am able to help but everything must sit correctly in place
before what you want can follow through. (I am I)

*

When you ask for advice listen, reassess and move forward.

*

I am waiting for you to choose your next move. (I am I)

*

I am the strength that you seek.
Still your thoughts so that we may link together. (I am I)

*

Don't you know how important you are to me? (I am I)

*

I will resolve this matter for you
but you must stay completely unbiased. (I am I)

*

Will you follow through
on your soul wisdom and higher purpose?

*

Everything is the way that it should be.

*

Each person is on their own voyage.
You have only to answer for your own.

How often do you think about me? (I am I)

*

No one can complete what you are destined to accomplish.

*

Why do you doubt what in fact you know to be true?

*

Life needs time to catch up. Time must also play its part.

*

You only can see your own part in this,
but the picture is larger and varied.

*

In the end nothing matters but love.

*

Today you are a trouble-free zone. (I am I)

*

In time you will know I am real. (I am I)

*

Everyone needs to be loved.

*

Not everyone feels the same as you, allow them to be themselves.

*

Why don't you try a new approach?

*

Each person will wake up in their own time
but, until that time occurs,
concentrate on your own habits, behaviour and growth.

*

You are human. Things happen.
What counts is how you choose to overcome them.

*

For this to work keep a positive mind
and focus on the outcome that you need to occur.

You are an un-blocker for life to follow through.
Be bold, be kind and be you.

*

There is no need to walk the same route as other people.
You have the knowledge and expertise to create your own.

*

What are you afraid of?
Don't you know who's rooting for you in higher realms?

*

Where are you heading?
What exactly is your intention and focus?

*

I am with you, so what are you asking of me? (I am I)

*

Be precise in your requests and with your aim.

*

Wait until you know the time is right.

*

No.

*

Money is a problem, but money is not all this is about.

*

Every obstacle reveals what still needs to be done.
Correct whatever necessary and try again.

*

I ask only that you give your very best.

*

Humanity is at a junction of progression or defeat.
Which way will you lead it through your example?

*

Work within the level of God, not within the level of man.
Love is the key to the knowledge that is yours to behold.
What this lesson will bring forth is up to you.

He who is the light cannot fail. (I am I)

*

Either you are positive, or you are not. You choose.

*

Do not be the judge of anyone or anything.
Down your gaze, clear your mind and work your day.

*

If we want the highest good, and we all play this right,
the highest good is precisely what we'll gain.

*

Miracles take time, but time is relative to only those on earth.
Keep the outcome in focus and all else as it must be in place.

*

I am with you; I know what you're thinking. (I am I)

*

*I am not able to move this on, it will depend on what is chosen
by other souls who interact. (I am I)*

*

I am abundance, peace, light and love manifested.
There is nothing I can't overcome.

*

*How many more ways must I show you that I love you,
that you are important to the world
and important to the life force that is me? (I am I)*

*

*I must tell you how to proceed, but to do this
you must keep your mind clutter free. (I am I)*

*

Why would I ever deny you exist? (I am I)

*

Who places my own needs higher than their own? Do you? (I am I)

*

Worry less, sing more. Feel healthy, happy and uplifted.

Let God be your first and last thought of the day.

*

All things are possible but first you must give them to God.

*

Come back to peace and let your soul soar,
that what is waiting can flow in unhampered.

*

We are beautifully linked. We live as one. (I am I)

*

Hold tight to your light (to right behaviour and good conduct)
to illuminate what has now to flow through.

*

Call upon God to assist you, every moment of every day,
that this power can indeed be your strength.

*

I am with God; we all are with God.
Understand and accept this now.

*

Have you considered where you fit in the big picture?

*

I am waiting for you to talk to me. (I am I)

*

What is your contribution to help the wider world?
What will you leave as the proof that you've been here?

*

If the journey was easy, humanity would be further forward.

*

Darkness and void do also exist.
Be mindful to remain in the light.

*

For the rest of your life, use it well.

*

Why do you doubt I can help you? (I am I)

Remember life is like a store cupboard;
you can only take out what first you have put in.

*

Reach back with your hand so that you can pull someone up.
I will walk with you and carry you forward when necessary. (I am I)

*

The world that you see was not all shaped by me but also by man.
I cannot override his free will. (I am I)

*

It will be fine, but in this now time you must worry less,
and you must trust.

*

This is the Garden of Eden.
No one is banished. All options are open.
It falls to you to choose how you go forward.

*

What is the meaning of life?
How are you replaying it back to me?
What you live, the way you think, what you do, good and bad,
you feed back to me as live input. (I am I)

*

Based on what you are thinking and saying,
how must I respond?
How must we together put this right? (I am I)

*

It will be successful!

*

Do you believe?

*

You write the programme of life.

*

What power you own comes from me.
You work, walk and talk on behalf of me.
Remember this fact as you move forward. (I am I)

What is it you think I have done? (I am I)

*

Why would you think I am not with you, even now?
How could you be lost and alone? (I am I)

*

The world needs you to work as its keeper
of balance and peace. (I am I)

*

Heaven is here.
Work on what must be done for the self and others,
so that you can be pleased at what you have achieved
through clearing and unblocking the path.

*

Help, as you too have been helped.

*

Don't worry what others may say about you.
Remain in the truth and move forward. (I am I)

*

You will be your own jury and judge at the end of your time here, not I.
Work the days that you have left with this in mind. (I am I)

*

Send healing down the time line of your past. (I am I)

*

Let go of the things you know you can't change from your past.
I will heal and recycle what you will reveal and relinquish.
Do not be the judge, for that falls to me.
I have stated already that you are forgiven.
Let go of the past.
Walk with me in Sunshine and Light. You walk free. (I am I)

*

That you are with me is not an illusion.
I will not wilfully force you away. (I am I)

I will take you forward.
Let go and let me.
Do nothing more.
Let time and my influence play their part. (I am I)

*

Don't practice your life, let it flow.

*

You cannot see the big picture
from the perspective of just your own viewpoint.
Trust that all will be as it should.

*

How can you know where this is heading?
As you work, let the whole thing unfold.

*

All you can see, all you think that you know,
is just a fraction of what is occurring on levels unseen.
We are working with you on your behalf. (I am I)

*

You are on the right path. Watch all thoughts carefully.
Let go of doubt. Don't sabotage yourself from within.

*

The task falls to you to help those who need help.
Take a moment to assess what must now come to pass.
Use your thoughts to request what is needed.

*

You do not need love; you are it.
You do not need courage for you are shielded by light.
You have all things in place,
for you are the now aspect of me. (I am I)

*

Wait and see. Don't force the issue.
Let all unfold according to the time it is meant to do so. (I am I)

*

How often do you let me speak through you? (I am I)

Honour the divine soul plan of another, regardless.

*

Be your divine perfect self at all times. Work with the
Ultimate Source as your truth and inspiration.

*

Why do you question what you know in your heart to be true?
Work from the heart, not the mind.

*

The Kingdom of Heaven is already inside your own being.
Either work with it, or not. The choice is always yours.

*

Turn away. Add no more to what is occurring.
You will be able to work through it later.

*

Will you be brave and follow my lead? (I am I)

Also by Stephanie J. King

And So It Begins...

You have more power over life than you realise

This is the first book written in a series destined to rebuild the hopes and happiness of man, who has thought himself unworthy and abandoned for far too long. Man is connected to the true source of life, to the source of the planet itself. He has never been anything other.

Man was born to live the life that is here now. This is his heritage, not his punishment. Man was meant to be happy, living his choices, not downtrodden and depressed. *And So It Begins...* mirrors aspects of character that rarely get considered. It helps unburden clutter, blindly passed down through generations, to gently reseat the deepest foundations. The time that each person has left and how he chooses to use it is the key to his future, and his future begins here - physically and spiritually 'now'. This is his legacy.

(I am I) How many people recognise my hand in life? How many under-stand that I know their every thought, wish and movement? How many realise I am not the vengeful ruling force they think me to be? How many wish for love and recognition but realise it is already within – just waiting to be unlocked and fully lived? (I am I)

And So It Begins... will take you by the hand and lead you forward in a way that is safe and realistic to be beneficial from the very first time that you use it. Every soul alive is born with a life agenda - chosen by him and higher beings - for his own soul's improvement. Each is on a journey of awakening and discovery. Each is placed in life where they can best achieve what needs to be accomplished and experienced.

Every soul, therefore every life, links directly to Earth, to Source, to the Universal Consciousness itself. *And So It Begins...* opens windows and doors to new insights and understanding that you may not have realised existed. Like an oracle/truth mirror/real-time life guide, it will quickly highlight your soul purpose and life agenda. You'll know exactly who you are, what you're part of, what's going on with others and life around you, what you're able to achieve and contribute, where and why things get stuck as well as ways you can effortlessly change this. You'll view differently past and present; your karma, talents, gifts and strengths, how others push your buttons and why you react - to stop repeating what you no longer need.

From teenager to elderly this book is already helping thousands to reassess what they've known, to rekindle dreams and goals, to turn life around and be happy. It highlights the negativities playing out in the present - to give you more choice and actually spins things around for the better... Read it as a book or dip into its pages (perfect for busy lifestyles), you'll actually feel yourself interacting with higher levels, with Source, with your own Spirit Guardian/Angel/Guide and with life - as if in direct conversation with a personal friend on a soul to soul level.

Empowered and completely in tune with where you are, you'll breeze through all aspects of life/love/work/family/home and move forward with ease, clearing clutter and blockages accumulated through generations and the years that you've personally been here - but make no mistake - this is not like any other book you have previously read for self-development. *And So It Begins...* will make a difference in your life and outlook right from the start... You'll feel healthier and happier with renewed energy and confidence, positivity, focus and life zest. This book is perfect for the already developed mind as well as for the beginner.

Helping you to also help others, you'll become a light worker - for what you give out will always come back. In this manner you'll help life heal itself.

(I am I) *The life force that is yours is unique. No one else can fill your shoes. No one else has had your same life experience. I need you to come back consciously to truths that wait here for you - to help ease your life 'now' and help you grow. (I am I)*

And So It Begins... can be used many times daily for up to the minute guidance that's completely in tune with what's happening around and about you, and as you receive this information - life will immediately respond in accordance. The help you need is here - the rest is up to you.

Life is Calling...

How to Manifest Your Life Plan

Are you aware that you're living a live real-time soul journey and that your limited time span here contains targets, purpose and goals? That you have talents, strengths and tasks to accomplish and contribute? That you were born with a pre-chosen life agenda of your own? That you've lived on earth before? That you create your own reality and that daily life needs and takes instructions straight from you? Do you know you connect to earth's own creative, thinking mind and that everything about you interacts?

Each day is a new day. It is another chance to create, to make a difference, to redraw and redefine who you are and what you do. How you live, interact and connect with daily life means every-thing - for all achievements you'll take with you, back to the realms of Spirit - as your contribution and offering to life, to physicality and to time.

Written like a deck of cards (with over 380 entries) but in an easy to manage book form, *Life is Calling...* was channelled by Spirit as a direct 'soul to soul' interchange. It's a link to advice for you from your own Guardian/Angel/Guide in a down to earth way that completely connects and relates to where you are. It will mirror everything as it highlights information that will prove relevant from the very first time that you use it.

Nothing happens by chance. You know everything about yourself, your thoughts, situations, history and events. You know what you believe in. Each time you pick it up Life is Calling... will correspond to now and be precise in the guidance, words and knowledge being given. It will completely turn around, balance and correct many things that you both consciously and subcon-sciously do - so you can choose and re- choose as you go along, depending on what's playing out.

Life is Calling... will help you manifest your own life plan step by step - and before long you will know exactly what that is and where you're heading... Labelled a phenomenon, this incredible inter-active book will take you by the hand and deliver specific, tailored guidance at the precise time and place you need it most. It can be surprising to realise how much you matter and that someone, something, somewhere, knows you better than you even know yourself, better than your own mother, loved ones, family and friends do - for your Guardian has always been with you - never judging, just helping and silently waiting for you to notice.

Perfect for busy lifestyles, this powerful guide book will help you to change much for the better, as you access higher truths and information that are with you.

Link and work directly with life's own creative forces. Interact with Source - as if being taken by the hand - so pure data, insights, inspiration, hunches and extrasensory information can filter through. Increase performance, optimise results, and reach targets and personal short and long term life goals easily, without an increase in effort from you - through renewed understanding and insight.

Love, work, family and home - all results will be immediate and immense.

This book has the potential to enhance the rest of your life - for the rest of the time frame that you live here.

Concise Pocket/Handbag Version

Due to popular demand - *Life is Calling...* is also now available in an abridged pocket/ handbag size/version. Many people love our book so much that nearly 200 entries 'specifically chosen by spirit' form this book - in a small easy to travel fashion size to see you through the day at random times...

'I Am' Meditations

Channelled Directly from Spirit

'I Am' is the first in a series of guided meditations unique in content and approach, allowing you to work directly with Source - to bring in health, balance, harmony, understanding, forgiveness, love, light, peace, growth and extra sensory infor- mation - from the highest realms - to aid all. Because your own journey is unique, your needs, questions and inspirations will be also...

Before birth we each devised a real-time soul agenda, an overall life plan, with live tasks to set in motion, to recognise and work through. We have qualities to contribute, to overcome and accomplish, gifts that we alone can hone and harness to feed directly back to life as personal input, as our contribution and thanks for time spent here.

Many things are answered as you reassess your lot - with the aid of personal guides/your guardian/and with Source. Physically, nothing is completely certain except we birth and die, yet far more occurs on levels unseen than we can ever imagine. The soul journey you are travelling is completely individual and unwritten - so what you will contribute, pay forward, or give back - is yours by personal choice and accomplishment...

Stephanie's works have been specifically channelled to help you work through karma and what's occurring now - love, work, family, home - to highlight what lies hidden, to fine tune your highest attributes, strengths and gifts, and to help you to regain, to remember what has been lost.

(I am I) I will work with you - if you will work with me. (I am I)

6th Books investigates the paranormal, supernatural, explainable or unexplainable. Titles cover everything included within parapsychology: how to, lifestyles, beliefs, myths, theories and memoir.